The Landsknechts: The History and Legacy of the German Mercenaries Who Fought for the Holy Roman Empire

By Charles River Editors

A 16th century depiction of Landsknechts

About the Author

Sean McLachlan is a historian and archaeologist who has explored ancient sites throughout Europe and the Middle East. He has written numerous books and articles on history and is also the author of several works of fiction, including the _Masked Man of Cairo_ series of historical mystery novels and the Civil War horror novel, _A Fine Likeness_. Learn more about his work on his Amazon page and Facebook page.

About Charles River Editors

Charles River Editors is a boutique digital publishing company, specializing in bringing history back to life with educational and engaging books on a wide range of topics. Keep up to date with our new and free offerings with this 5 second sign up on our weekly mailing list, and visit Our Kindle Author Page to see other recently published Kindle titles.

We make these books for you and always want to know our readers' opinions, so we encourage you to leave reviews and look forward to publishing new and exciting titles each week.

Introduction

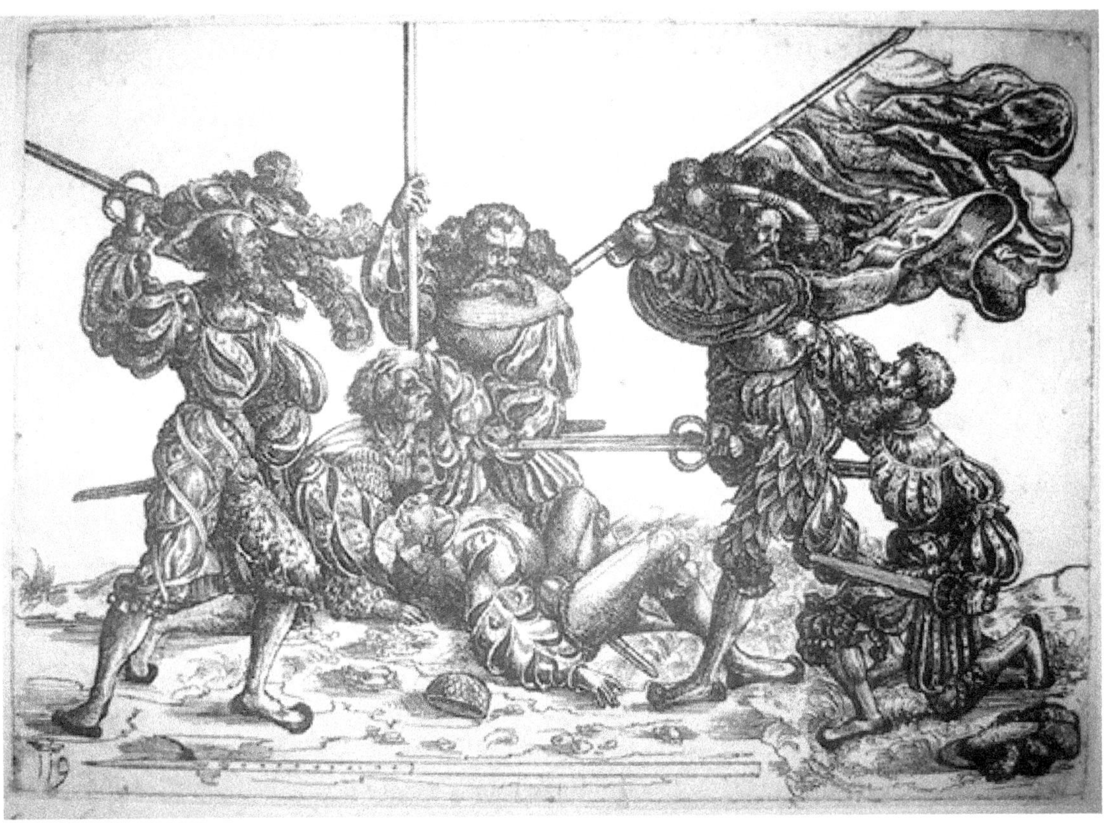

A 16th century etching depicting a flag bearer fighting Landsknechts

When historians are asked to pick a point in history when Western Civilization was transformed and guided down the path to modernity, most of them point to the Renaissance. Indeed, the period revolutionized art, philosophy, religion, sciences and math, with individuals like Galileo, Leonardo, Michelangelo, Raphael, Dante, and Petrarch bridging the past and modern society. The Renaissance also spawned the use of the label "Renaissance Man" to describe a person who is extremely talented in multiple fields, most notably Leonardo da

Vinci, who found time to be a painter, sculptor, architect, musician, scientist, mathematician, engineer, inventor, anatomist, geologist, cartographer, botanist, and writer.

However, while the Renaissance is remembered mostly for art and advances in philosophy and thinking, it's often overlooked that the era was also a transitional period in the history of warfare. The Middle Ages have long been remembered for armored knights battling on horseback and armies of men trying to breach the walls of formidable castles, but what is generally forgotten is that medieval warfare was constantly adapting to the times as leaders adopted new techniques and technology, and common infantry became increasingly important throughout the period. Meanwhile, political and technological progress led to continuous change of tactics and equipment. Cavalry became ascendant, only to be later replaced by infantry as their weapons improved, and by the end of the period, warfare was radically changing thanks to the rise of gunpowder weapons such as the handgonne and the bombard.

Artillery and handgonnes had been known since the early 14th century but only became effective near the end of the 15th century, when they were the final factor in the infantry revolution and began to change warfare forever. By the middle of the 15th century, artillery was knocking down castle walls that had stood for generations. Infantry also proved their worth with powerful longbows and tight formations of polearms upsetting the long dominance of mounted, heavily armored knights, and handheld firearms threatened to make armor obsolete. New types of warriors were developed, and new tactics had to take the emerging era of black powder weapons into account, ushering in a time of great change in military strategy, tactics, and technology.

The Middle Ages witnessed almost constant warfare in Europe, so mercenaries were a constant on the battlefield, but the 15th century also saw the rise of mercenary usage by the increasingly wealthy aristocracy. One of the finest groups of mercenaries were the Landsknechts from central and northern Europe. The term means "servant of the country," and they mostly served the Holy Roman Empire, first under Emperor Maximilian I (r. 1508-1519) and then under his successors. The Landsknechts (German: *Landsknechte*) were masters of the battlefield, adept at pike, sword, and dead shots with the crude matchlocks of the day. The only mercenaries rivaling them were the famous Swiss, who they hated and often fought bitterly. The Landsknechts were as famous for their flamboyant costumes as much as their prowess on the battlefield, and they became symbols of rebellion and freedom in early modern Europe, even as they fought in service of Europe's largest empire.

The Landsknechts: The History and Legacy of the German Mercenaries Who Fought for the Holy Roman Empire examines the events that led to the rise of the mercenaries, what their lives and battles were like, and their impact. Along with pictures depicting important people, places, and events, you will learn about the Landsknechts like never before.

Medieval Warfare

In the 14th century, medieval warfare started to change from being dominated by cavalry to giving a larger role, and eventually a dominant role, to the infantry. Several weapons were key to what historians often call the "infantry revolution," including longbows, crossbows, pikes, handgonnes, and polearms.

A polearm is a staff weapon that has a head that can perform more than one function, such as cutting, chopping, impaling, or pulling an enemy off his horse. One of the most common and longest-lived type of polearm is the halberd, which can chop and impale. It made its first appearance at the Battle of Morgarten on November 15, 1315. Austrian knights advanced through a Swiss pass and were ambushed by Swiss fighters using halberds, attacking from the rocks above. The knights were slaughtered and the halberd became a standard Swiss weapon for centuries. It's still carried today by the Pope's Swiss Guard.

David Ball's picture of reenactors with halberds

Polearms proved effective in many battles and were a

mainstay of the armies during the Wars of the Roses. Using a simple polearm adapted from a branch cutter, they could unhorse knights and cleave through armor. Like the Swiss halberdiers, they fought in formation. Unlike pikemen, however, a single man bearing a polearm was still dangerous, while pikemen needed large numbers and a tight formation to be effective.

Pikes were iron-headed spears with shafts measuring from 14 to 18 feet. Seasoned ash was the favored wood as it was strong and flexible. This heavy, awkward weapon required a great deal of training to be used properly. Entire military manuals were dedicated to a complex set of drills for using pikes in formation, although in battle, there were generally only a few movements used. The Swiss were so well-trained that pike squares of up to 10,000 men could maneuver across the battlefield with ease.

For holding the line against a cavalry charge, the men in the front rank would crouch with the butt of the pike resting against the right instep while holding the pike at an angle that put the point level with the horse's breast. This stance was called "charge for horse." The second rank, and sometimes a couple more ranks behind them, held their pikes in the "charged" position, with one hand gripping the butt-end of the pike while the other gripped the shaft.

For fighting against fellow infantry, the front three to five ranks held their pikes level in the "charged" position. The rear ranks held their pikes at an angle above their comrades' heads in the front ranks. If a man fell, the file of men of which he was a part moved forward a rank so the space would be filled.

Pike formations were first developed by the Swiss in the 15th century, loosely based on similar formations in ancient Greece. Just as the Greeks strengthened their hoplite pike formations with archers and slingers on the flanks, the Swiss had highly-trained crossbowmen and handgonners firing at the enemy in an attempt to break their formation and keep enemy archers and handgonners at bay.

Another important weapon in the infantry revolution was the crossbow. The crossbow harkens back to Roman times, when large examples called *ballistae* were used in sieges and to send large bolts cutting through enemy formations. Handheld crossbows existed too as a hunting weapon. Smaller handheld crossbows reappeared in medieval Europe in the 11th century as a military weapon, especially among the Normans and Spanish. While they were more powerful and easier to use than the bows at the time (the longbow had yet to make its appearance) they did not replace bows because they were all but impossible to aim beyond about 80 yards. The trouble was that any bolt or arrow flies in an arc due to the pull of gravity, so firing at anything beyond that range required tilting the crossbow upwards so much it obscured the view of the target.

Another weapon vital to the infantry revolution was the longbow, which has already been mentioned in several of the battles already discussed. While the bow was used throughout ancient times and the Middle Ages, on mainland Europe it was mostly replaced by the crossbow in the early 13th century. This would change with the introduction of the longbow, a more powerful weapon than the traditional hunting bows. The original longbowmen were Welshmen recruited by King Edward I of England after he conquered Wales.

The weapon got its name from the fact that it was almost as tall as the man using it. This gave it a longer draw and therefore more force. Longbows were generally made of yew, a strong and pliable wood. The longbow was cheap and easy to make, but required extensive training to be used well.

In the 14th century, the old feudal levies began to be replaced with methodical enlistment for regular pay. Feudal levies were always unreliable for long campaigns since there was a natural desire to return home to take care of the fields. Short forays into enemy territory could be profitable, but no one wanted to miss planting or harvest. Soldiers being paid a regular wage were more likely to stay, and in the 15th century standing armies began to become the norm.

The main purpose of most campaigns was booty. The land would be ravaged, stripped of its valuables, its buildings burned, and its fields laid to waste. This weakened the enemy at planting time and made it more difficult for them to launch their own campaign. Commanders often avoided an open battle as these could be risky. If too many of the nobility got killed, it would seriously weaken the kingdom and cause internal strife. Leaders would try to fool the enemy as to their intentions, and if a battle seemed unavoidable, try to catch the enemy by surprise.

The nobility would not be riding their best horses on the march. Instead they would ride ordinary horses in order to keep their best warhorses rested for any battle. Likewise, neither they nor the regular troops would wear armor unless contact with the enemy seemed imminent.

Armies would march and fight in three main divisions— the vanguard, the main guard, and the rearguard. The vanguard would be in front, the main guard or *bataille* in the center, while the rearguard took up the rear and protected the wagon train. These three main units stayed the same even in battle, having set places on the line.

  While pitched battles have always caught the imagination of the chroniclers, artists, and modern historians, they were in fact quite rare until about 1300. In fact, they were generally fought only as a last resort to stop an invasion. Battles were risky affairs, where important members of one's ruling class could be killed or permanently disabled. At Bannockburn in 1314, the English nobility lost somewhere between 154 and 700 of its members. At Crécy, more than 1,200 knights lost their lives, including nine princes. More than 15,000 other ranks also died, but that was less important in the minds of the nobility. Almost as bad, and far more common since battles often had a low mortality rate, were the nobles lost to capture, for they would subsequently be ransomed for exorbitant amounts.

  Sieges were a better way to capture territory. The pioneering work of military historian Jim Bradbury specified the "six S's of siege warfare:" suborning or subverting key defenders, scaring the garrisons with propaganda, sapping the walls, starving the population, storming the defenses, and shelling the defenders. Cities, not castles, were the main focus of siege warfare because cities offered wealth and a taxable population. Castles were often set at key geographic points so that invading armies would have to invest them.

A siege required preparations on both sides. Many siege engines included complex parts that had to be made beforehand and brought with the invading army. Foragers would spread out across the countryside to secure as much food as possible for the inevitable waiting game with the defenders.

For their part, defenders would strip the surrounding countryside of all food, fuel, and forage in order to shorten the time the attackers could stay in the region. They would also send out sallies to harass the attackers and destroy important siege engines and artillery.

As with the infantry and cavalry, there was an arms race between armies and castle builders. Castles at the beginning of our period were simple affairs, generally wooden stockades with a ditch. The Normans were masters at this sort of fortification in the 11th century. Their motte-and-bailey castles consisted of an area enclosed by a wooden stockade, plus an artificial hill also enclosed by its own stockade and holding up a wooden tower. The whole fortification would be surrounded by a ditch. Motte-and-bailey castles were quick and cheap to construct and were widely used after the battle of Hastings in 1066 to secure the English countryside. The Anglo-Saxons, having no siege engines, found it difficult to take them.

As time went on, many of the wooden towers and walls of the more important motte-and-bailey castles were replaced with stone. Stone castles developed elsewhere in Europe too. At first they were simple square keeps with surrounding walls and a wet or dry moat to add another level of protection. Towers were set on the corners, pushing out from the line of the walls to allow archers crossfire against anyone trying to storm the walls. Arrow slits were set at regular intervals in the towers and walls and the walls themselves were topped with crenellations, a jagged series of stones that allowed the defenders to hide while reloading their bows.

Various other siege engines were used to bombard enemy fortifications. The simplest was the catapult. These were wooden arms on frames that would be pulled back using torsion to build up potential energy. The end of the beam had a shallow bowl that held a stone or bundle of flaming pitch. When the torsion was released, the beam would snap up and be stopped at 90 degrees by a crossbeam. The missile would then fly forward. A number of these could batter at the walls or throw stones into the city beyond. Incendiary devices could start a fire inside that would demoralize the defenders and hasten their surrender. Fire was always a danger in crowded medieval cities, but attackers would think twice about burning down a city they wanted to make their own.

A more powerful stone thrower was the trebuchet, which was a large beam with a heavy counterweight. The beam would be pulled down and let go, and the counterweight would make the end of the beam fly up. A sling on the end of the beam would then release a stone. Trebuchets were often quite large and the chronicles say that the largest could throw stones weighing up to 350 pounds. A modern reconstruction at Warwick Castle in England weighs 22 tons, stands 59 feet tall, and can throw an 80 pound stone up to 980 feet.

Luc Viatour's picture of a trebuchet

Gunpowder

Gunpowder was invented in China in the 8th or 9th century AD, and its use slowly spread through South Asia and the Middle East before making it to Europe in the late 13th century. The famous scholar Francis Bacon gave a recipe for it in a book written in 1267, but for a time it was a mere curiosity. The first record of a cannon in Europe comes from a manuscript written in 1326, which has an illustration showing an armored man with what looks like a slow match lighting a vase-shaped object. An arrow is shooting out of the opening. This crude cannon was called a *pot de fer* in French and *vasi* in Italian. A small specimen weighing 20 pounds has survived in Sweden and is 12 inches long with a 1.5 inch bore. Records show they fired large iron or wooden quarrels with metal fins halfway along the shaft. The rear of the shaft would have been padded to better contain the expanding gases of the exploding powder.

Eventually, medieval engineers developed a new type of cannon in the form of a large cylinder made up of iron bars fused together and strengthened with hoops like a barrel. In fact, this is where the term for the "barrel" of a gun comes from. These devices were called *cannons* or *bombards*. The arrow was replaced with a sphere of stone or lead, both materials being cheap and easy to work. These cannon balls proved to be more aerodynamic and generated more impact than the old-style arrows.

Cannons were quickly brought into use both for sieges and pitched battles. The earliest reference to cannons being used in sieges was the siege of Friuli in Italy in 1331, but it's unclear when they were first used in the field. They may have been used at the battle of Crécy in 1346. It is certain that both the English and French armies were equipped with cannons, but none of the eyewitness accounts of the battle mention them, only a few later histories written decades later.

Bombards grew in size, with some reaching epic proportions. For these giant cannons, the balls would be made of stone because using so much lead would have been prohibitively expensive. This increase in size was encouraged by the development of cheaper gunpowder. Until the late 14th century, saltpeter, a key ingredient in gunpowder, had to be imported from India or found in the rare natural conditions that encouraged its formation. By the end of the 14th century, Europeans had figured out how to make their own saltpeter and production increased to industrial levels.

Large bombards proved effective at knocking down castle walls. The first recorded instance of this was at the siege of Saint-Sauveur-le-Vicomte in 1375, and cases are frequent thereafter. It is interesting to note that the siege of Saint-Sauveur-le-Vicomte used 200 pounds of gunpowder, an impossibly lavish supply before prices for gunpowder dropped. Soon supplies of gunpowder for sieges and campaigns would be measured in the thousands of pounds.

While thick walls, curved towers, and sallies by the defenders to destroy the besieging artillery kept early artillery from being a game changer for quite some time, as soon as the walls of Saint-Sauveur-le-Vicomte crumbled, the days of castles and walled cities were numbered. Even so, reducing a fortified position remained a major undertaking. The 1466 siege of Dinant in Belgium took a week and 1,700 shots. Sometimes attackers ran out of powder or shot, which happened to the Burgundians at their 1475 siege of Cologne.

**A picture indicating some of the damage done to
Saint-Sauveur-le-Vicomte**

It wasn't long after the invention of artillery that gunners
began to experiment with smaller, handheld black powder
weapons. Cannons had the great disadvantage of being

slow and cumbersome. There are several reports of artillery not making it to the battle on time, and even the *ribaudiaux* moved more slowly than the average soldier could march. The solution, of course, was to create a small black powder weapon that could be carried by a single man.

European sources first mentioned the widespread use of handgonnes, as they were often called, in the late 14th century, precisely the time when gunpowder became cheaper. These were short metal barrels stuck on the end of wooden hafts that could be tucked under the arm, the powder being lit through a touchhole with the free hand. While they were not terribly accurate, and had a shorter range and slower rate of fire than longbows or crossbows, they had the advantage of being better able to punch through armor than longbows and crossbows. A second advantage was that they were simple to make and use.

Another type of handgonne was the *hackbut*, or hook gun. These generally had long metal stocks fused directly with the barrel. On the bottom of the barrel was a hook that could be braced against a pavise or wall in order to steady the gun and allow more accurate firing. Since they were designed to be braced, *hackbuts* could be larger than regular handgonnes.

Peasants were using handgonnes right from the start.

When a group of revolting peasants attacked Huntercombe Manor in England in 1375, they carried with them several handgonnes, and handgonnes soon became a common weapon in peasant rebellions and for urban militias. As cities grew in the 14th century, these militias could be quite large. The one of Strasburg is recorded in 1392 as having 20,000 fully armed men ready for action at a moment's notice. Of course, cities would also be centers of gunpowder and handgonne production.

Handgonnes were limited by their small caliber and modest charge of powder. Early gunpowder was not very powerful, another reason that cannons grew steadily larger in size. Around the beginning of the 15th century, however, chemists developed crumbled and corned powder. By wetting the powder slightly and patting it into a cake to be left to dry, the gunpowder could be stored without the ingredients getting separated or absorbing too much moisture. Not only could it be stored longer than early gunpowder, it could then be crumbled into a large-grain powder with higher surface-to-volume ratio that made it burn quicker. This greatly increased the explosive force.

The earliest handgonnes were tucked under the arm and lit manually with a slow match that touched the gunpowder in the priming pan before lighting the main charge in the barrel. Such an awkward firing stance made aiming difficult. Later, a simple lever device held the slow match, called a serpentine. Pressing the level brought the slow match down on the firing pan. This was soon replaced with an actual trigger, and the soldier was able to bring the gun up to his shoulder and look down the barrel, vastly improving the soldier's ability to aim. This gun was called the *arquebus*, and it was the first black powder firearm that looked like a modern rifle. It appeared by the end of the 15th century but was still a cumbersome piece with a barrel measuring three to four-and-a-half feet long with a heavy stock. Arquebusiers used a "rest"—a short pole with a spike that stuck in the earth and a u-shaped rest, similar to an oarlock—to hold the arquebus. As matchlock muskets developed into lighter, more manageable weapons, the forked rest was gradually discarded.

There is some confusion with the terms "arquebus" and "musket," with contemporaries and modern writers sometimes using them interchangeably. The first muskets were actually bigger than the arquebus. By the mid-17th century, however, the term "musket" was generally used for lighter firearms that didn't require rests. By the end of that century, the musket had all but replaced the arquebus, and soldiers carrying firearms were now referred to as musketeers.

The arquebus had an effective range of 50-60 yards. The

ball traveled further, but beyond that distance, hitting was a matter of pure chance. A trained arquebusier could fire every 30-60 seconds. By contrast, the matchlock musket had an effective range of between 100-120 yards, and as it was lighter, it had a slightly faster rate of fire.

To improve the slow rate of fire, arquebusiers wore a bandolier belt with a dozen leather tubes containing measured charges of gunpowder, which the men jokingly referred to as the "Twelve Apostles." A separate bag held the bullets, but in battle, the men often kept the bullets in their mouths to have quicker access to them. The lead turned their lips and teeth green and probably undermined their health.

The matchlock had another disadvantage: the slow match could easily be snuffed out in the rain or even a heavy mist, and a damp slow match couldn't be lit, so it was unreliable in inclement weather. If they expected rain, arquebusiers kept their spare, unlit slow matches under their hats, giving us the expression "keep it under your hat."

Another development was the wheellock, a wound-up, flint-and-steel mechanism that, when the trigger was pulled, spun like a modern lighter, sending sparks into the firing pan. This was no faster to reload than a matchlock, and its complicated mechanism meant that it often misfired. On the other hand, the mechanism made little movement to disrupt aim, and thus was quite accurate for its day.

In pistol and carbine form, wheel locks were also used by cavalry, who didn't have spare hands to manipulate slow matches. Each cavalryman often carried two or more wheel locks, and in the 16th century, a tactic emerged, called the "caracole," in which riders approached slow-moving infantry formations—such as pike squares—in columns. The first rank fired their pistols or carbines and wheel to the left or right to be replaced by the next rank. Thus, a steady, if not particularly accurate, fire could be kept up against the infantry, at least until the riders ran out of shots and had to move away from the fighting to reload their guns. If the enemy was sufficiently broken up by the fire, the cavalry, who were armored and carried swords, could charge at the enemy and try to finish them off. The German Reiters were some of the pioneers of this tactic, starting in the 1540s.

Students of military history will recognize the caracole maneuver as an updated version of methods used by horse archers, such as the Parthians and Mongols. Ancient accounts of battles were avidly read by Renaissance military theorists and leaders, and the lessons learned centuries before were reintroduced with updated technology.

It would not be until the full adoption of the matchlock and further improvements in gunpowder that full plate armor would disappear. Armor was still useful against other weapons, and until the full development of the matchlock, handgonnes remained inaccurate, short-range devices. They tended to be used in conjunction with other weapons, with handgonners most commonly being teamed up with crossbowmen. Crossbows were more accurate and had a faster rate of fire, and although crossbow bolts were less likely to punch through armor, they could provide a good covering fire, harassing and slowly diminishing the enemy until they got close enough for the handgonners to deliver a deadly volley.

Handgonnes, even in their simple form, spread quickly throughout Europe. Many castle owners modified the arrow slits on their walls, cutting circular holes in them to accommodate handgonnes or small cannons. By the late 15th century, handgonners had become a major part of the leading armies. An account about the army from Milan in 1482 mentions 1,250 handgonners, 233 crossbowmen, and 352 arquebusiers. The arquebus was expensive to make, so for a time the more primitive handgonnes remained in use for the bulk of the men, but crossbows were clearly on their way out.

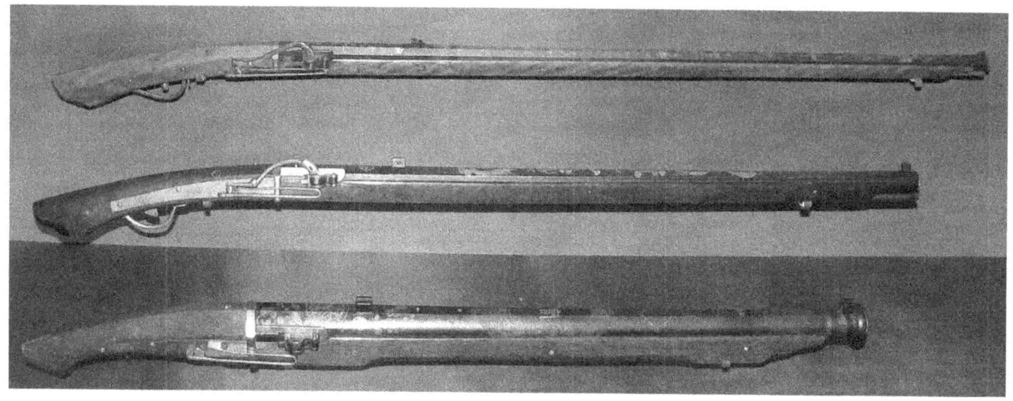

A picture of Italian arquebuses

The most effective early use of handgonnes and artillery was by the Hussites in their rebellion against the Holy Roman Empire from 1419-1436. This was an army composed mostly of peasants and civilians from small towns in the Czech homeland, strengthened by the retinues of a few rebellious nobles. They were fighting for their independence against an advanced and experienced army.

Knowing they couldn't defeat the Holy Roman Empire in a simple fight on the open field, the Hussites used their rural resources and skills to the utmost advantage. Their principal innovation was the *wagenburg,* a moving wall of fortified farm wagons with wooden planks fastened to their sides fitted with firing holes. Archers, crossbowmen, and handgonners could fire from them in relative safety. Some wagons were equipped with cannons. The wagons could be chained together and drawn into a circle to make a fortress that could be easily disassembled and moved elsewhere.

Each wagon was equipped with tools in order to dig entrenchments and was manned by two drivers, two handgonners, six crossbowmen, fourteen men with flails, four men with halberds, and two men carrying pavises. The pavisiers would block off the spaces between wagons and give the crossbowmen and handgonners not in the wagons themselves a space from behind which to shoot.

As can be seen, much of the equipment was readily available in any peasant village—flails, digging tools, and carts. Handgonnes and halberds were easy enough for the village blacksmith to make. Crossbows and gunpowder required specialized labor to make but little training to use.

The Hussites used their wagenburgs in a tactic of offensive defense. They would wheel the mobile fortress near an important road or town, circle the wagons, and wait. The enemy, faced with having the Hussites near some key point, would have no choice but to attack. Fighting from behind fortified wagons, the Hussites negated most of the advantage enjoyed by mounted knights. This tactic worked so well that other armies began to adopt it. Within a couple of generations, however, more mobile and powerful artillery made the wagenburgs vulnerable and they were discarded.

Charles the Bold

Charles the Bold

Arguably the most advanced army before the start of the 16th century was that of Charles the Bold, Duke of Burgundy, who ruled from 1467-1477. He tried to unify his fragmented kingdom by buying up the best soldiers he could, including mounted forces, English longbowmen, Italian condottieri as armored cavalry and infantry crossbowmen, handgonners, and pikemen. The army was highly organized and blended different types of soldiers to take advantage of their best aspects while compensating for each other's weaknesses. His pike formations were mixed with archers and handgonners to provide covering fire and drive away enemies shooting at the formation. Likewise, mounted longbowmen rode with the heavy armored cavalry to provide covering fire from the flanks.

The most advanced wing of Charles the Bold's army was the artillery train. The falcon cannon looked much more like a modern artillery piece than the earlier bombards. Mounted on a wheeled wooden frame with an adjustable barrel, it offered much more maneuverability and accuracy than any competing artillery.

By the 1470s, however, Charles the Bold began to meet his match, despite the fact the Burgundian army was the most advanced in Europe. It boasted a large number of feudal lords in full armor, levied a gentry that included many knights and tough mercenaries, all of which were well-organized under a tight command structure. It was a modern army, highly trained with an organized artillery train of the most advanced cannons available. But the Swiss beat the Burgundians at the Battle of Héricourt on November 13, 1474. Burgundian casualties were recorded as 1,617 dead, a large number for what had been a small engagement. Interestingly, the Burgundian force did not have their famous artillery train with them, but both sides had units of handgonners, who fired crude handheld firearms.

The Burgundians suffered defeat again at the much larger Battle of Grandson on March 2, 1476. Both armies numbered about 20,000, and this time the Burgundians had their artillery with them, but they only fired a few shots because the Swiss pikemen advanced remarkably rapidly to engage the Burgundian infantry and cavalry. The Burgundians were unable to get through the line of pikes, and as their artillery was unable to support them at such close quarters, they soon fled, leaving their camp to be plundered. The Swiss also captured many of their guns, some of which are still on display in Swiss museums.

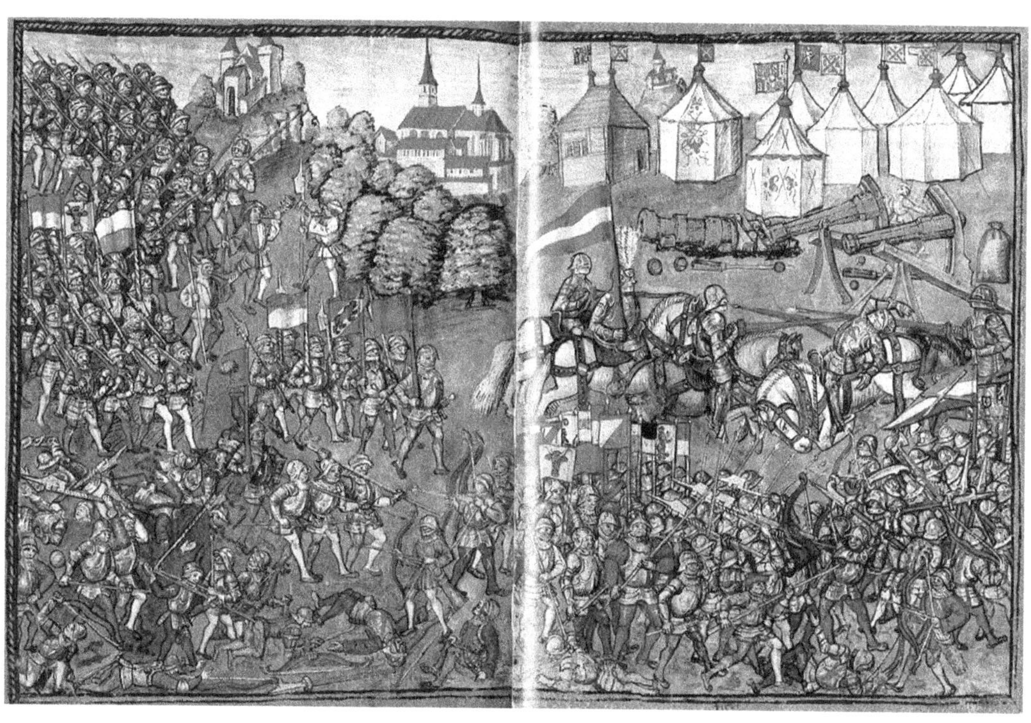

A 16th century illustration of the battle

Charles the Bold's next defeat came on June 22, 1476 at the Battle of Morat. This time, the Swiss outnumbered the Burgundians, but Charles (who was starting to be known as Charles the Rash) engaged anyway. Charles besieged the city of Morat, held by the Swiss Confederation, and gradually reduced it to rubble with artillery, but when he heard of the approach of a Swiss relief force, he met it in hilly terrain, making the Swiss pike squares less effective. The Swiss marched from this direction and had no choice but to pass through the unfavorable terrain. To further strengthen his position, Charles had his men dig ditches and ramparts, positioning archers and artillery behind them, with one flank being secured by a steep gorge.

The Swiss arrived late, but since it was payday, many Burgundians who were supposed to be guarding the earthworks were back at camp in a disorganized mass, trying to get their money and settle down to eat lunch. The skeleton crew at the earthworks was completely surprised by the unexpected arrival of the Swiss, and though they held on for a time, they were seriously outnumbered and finally broke. The Swiss reformed beyond the earthworks and marched into the Burgundian camp.

The Burgundians tried to rally, but the units were scattered, and they attacked the compact pike square piecemeal and were knocked aside, one by one. Charles had to retreat once again, leaving his camp's equipment behind him.

The final blow came in northeastern France on January 5, 1477. On that day, Charles the Bold led some 8,000 men, although some estimates put his numbers much lower. Facing him were about 12,000 French and 10,000 Swiss.

Once again, Charles besieged a city, this time the city of Nancy, the capital of Lorraine. When the Swiss and French relief force approached, Charles took up position on a heavily wooded slope behind a stream in a narrow valley. He had with him some 30 field guns, but a driving snowstorm reduced visibility to only a few yards, making the guns all but useless.

Despite the poor visibility, the French and Swiss forces had scouted out their position and engaged the Burgundians with a direct assault with a part of their force, while the main force struggled through hilly and wooded terrain to flank the defenders on the left. The force emerged from the woods uphill from the Burgundians and charged down at them.

Charles rallied his men, and they fought bravely but were seriously outnumbered and nearly surrounded. Units melted away as Charles bemoaned the fact that he "struggle[d] against a spider who [was] everywhere at once."

As his formations were broken into smaller and smaller units, Charles found himself isolated with a small number of men, surrounded by attacking Swiss. One Swiss fighter hit Charles on the head with a halberd, breaking through his helmet and killing him. The slaughter was such that it took three days to pick through the bodies to find Charles the Bold, once a feared general but now a symbol of a dying age.

This remarkable series of defeats shows how a well-organized and technologically advanced army could not stand up to innovative infantry tactics. Theoretically, the Burgundian artillery should have been able to blast large holes through the tightly formed pike squares, but they ended up being no match for them. No doubt, the Swiss did suffer losses from artillery fire, but their highly trained pikemen were able to quickly shift location within the square to plug any gaps and advance rapidly enough that the slow-loading cannons could only get off a couple of shots before the pikemen were upon them.

The secret to his enemies' success was the *Reisläufer*, Swiss mercenaries (mostly pikemen) who were poorly disciplined and lacked a strong overall command structure, but were highly trained and motivated in battle. They came from the many independent cantons making up the Helvetic Confederation in what would become Switzerland, and though Switzerland is now a centralized nation, at the time it was a place of constant low-level fighting between cantons and neighboring villages. The young men were well-accustomed to brawling, and each village was drilled with the pike and other weapons to stand against more serious attacks.

This was the key to the Swiss' strength. Not only were they highly trained in the use of the pike, halberd, short sword, and dagger, but they were also fiercely loyal to the men beside them, who were their friends, neighbors, and relatives. This created a far more cohesive unit than a bunch of people drawn up by feudal levy and led by some noble to whom the men had never spoken. The Swiss, on the other hand, were led by the *schultheiss*, a local noble with a much closer relationship to the men than his lowland counterparts. Sometimes, the schultheiss wasn't nobility at all, but some local hero who had risen to prominence through ability and charisma.

The Origins of the Landsknechts

After the death of Charles the Bold, Burgundy came into the hands of Archduke Maximilian I von Habsburg of the Holy Roman Empire, who inherited Burgundy in 1477 by marrying Mary, Duchess of Burgundy. Mary was the only child of Charles the Bold, and she retained her role as duchess even after marrying Maximilian. A shrewd politician who wanted to ensure Burgundy's freedom against French expansionism, she married Maximilian to protect her land. It was a good deal for Maximilian, too, since Burgundy had some of the richest farmlands and cities in Europe. Indeed, his new wife was often referred to as Mary the Rich.

Maximilian I

Mary, Duchess of Burgundy

There were many threats to the expanding Holy Roman Empire. Not only did France contest Maximilian's inheritance, but the Ottoman Empire threatened in the east, there was a wave of peasant rebellions all over Europe, and smaller fights were going on in Sweden and Italy. With all that in mind, Maximilian set out to reorganize the empire's combined militaries along Swiss lines while retaining the famous Burgundian artillery, and his new reforms were quickly put to the test in 1479, when the French King Louis XI (r. 1461-1483) contested

Mary's inheritance of Burgundy. Maximilian levied a Flemish Army and met a large French force on August 7 of that year at Guinegate in the county of Artois in what is now northern France. At that time, it was nominally a Burgundian territory recently taken by the French.

Maximilian led his men against the French that day, but while this was normal practice, he did not ride into battle on horseback, as was typical of nobility. Instead, he and about 200 other nobles fought on foot as a part of two massive pike squares in the center of the Imperial line. This was the first time pike squares had been used by troops who were not Swiss. The line was flanked on either side by the Burgundian cavalry.

The French also had their cavalry on the flanks and their infantry in the middle, but their infantry was mostly armed with bows, crossbows, and regular hand-to-hand weapons. They also only fielded about half the number of the Imperial army.

The French did well initially, as their cavalry drove off the Imperial left flank and captured the artillery in that position, turning the guns on the Imperial center. However, the impetuous French knights subsequently threw away their advantage by pursuing the Imperial knights and leaving the field at a crucial time. The Imperial pike squares then pressed forward, destroying the

French center while the remaining French cavalry was unable to break through the wall of pikes, and the French were forced to retreat, yielding the field to Maximilian.

By using Swiss tactics, Archduke Maximilian had defeated the French force and secured Burgundy for his wife. Mary died a few years later in 1482, and it fell to Maximilian to continue reorganizing the military on both his and her land. While his victory at Guinegate had staved off the French for a time, peace never reigned for long in that era. His Flemish levies had gone home after the campaign, and the French had cornered the market on Swiss Reisläufer, so Maximilian needed a permanent standing army and a reliable mercenary force to rival his enemies on the battlefield.

At that time, no land could sustain a large, permanent force like the kind found today, so mercenaries were essential, but Maximilian needed mercenaries that couldn't be lured away by his enemies. Thus, in 1486, he formed a band of mercenaries drawn from young German men from within the Holy Roman Empire. In the first year, he raised as many as 8,000 of them and dubbed them Landsknechts, which means "servant of the land." The idea was that despite the fact they were mercenaries, they would only hire out to the Holy Roman Emperor or its approved allies. Maximilian ordered them to be trained as Swiss pikemen, giving them charismatic leaders who encouraged personal loyalty and *esprit de corps*.

Mercenaries have historically been depicted as unreliable and possessing no loyalty to their employers beyond wages, and while that was often true, mercenary bands were loyal to themselves. In a tough world where nothing was certain, the men who responded to the call for mercenaries were often those with no ties to family or land. Many were out of work or second sons who would never inherit a shop or enough land to support themselves. Some, no doubt, came from war-ravaged areas and had already lost everything. Within the mercenary band, these men found a home and camaraderie with similar men on whom they could rely. The genius of the Landsknecht organization was that it fostered such strong feelings.

One of the earliest and best units of the Landsknechts was the "Black Guard," formed in Bruges in 1487 and commanded by Eitel Friedrich II, Count of Hohenzollern. Using Swiss instructors, the men became experts at pike formations. They fought with distinction throughout Northern Germany and Denmark and were often used to put down the frequent peasant rebellions of the time.

Eitel Friedrich II

In 1488, Maximilian raised the first Landsknecht army in Germany, the Swabian League, made up of 12,000 infantry and 1,200 cavalry to deter threats from Bavaria and Bohemia. At that time, the Holy Roman Empire was a patchwork of duchies, principalities, and free cities, which meant that even though Maximilian wanted to rule like a monarch, he was hampered by the privileges each small state and city enjoyed. Most were Imperial Estates, meaning they had representation and the right to vote in the Imperial Diet (*Reichstag*). As such, they enjoyed a great deal of autonomy, although they did recognize the emperor as overall ruler. The Swabian League thus represented a successful attempt by Maximilian to form a mutual defense treaty to deal with imminent threats in one region of the empire. Left to their own defenses, individual Imperial Estates were weak, and the rest, while nominally required to come to each other's aid, might move too slowly.

The Swabian League's coat of arms

One of the first big tests for the Landsknechts came during the brief Hungarian War, which started in 1490. Maximilian wanted to retake parts of Hungary after they had been captured by the Hungarians during the reign of his father, Frederick III (r. 1452-1493). Using the death of Matthias I, the king of Hungary and Croatia (r. 1458-1490), as an excuse, he marched into Hungary with an army of 20,000 men, mostly Landsknechts, and enjoyed a series of victories, culminating in the storming of the Bohemian fortress of Stuhlweissenburg.

Maximilian's next objective was Budapest, but his Landsknechts, upset over not having been paid, dispersed and went home. They had already made enough money by looting the towns and countryside and saw no reason for any further fighting. Maximilian now understood that he needed to create a more cohesive, organized force on which he could rely for extended campaigns.

The Organization of the Landsknechts

One of the Landsknechts' distinguishing characteristics was their high degree of organization. Along with the fighters, there were a large number of officers and special officials who kept order in camp and made sure the baggage train and camp followers didn't slow the army down or get in the way. And despite their reputation as merciless bruisers, the Landsknechts were highly disciplined, except when looting enemy territories (or friendly territories if they hadn't been paid in a while).

While Maximilian's new armies were recruited based on ability rather than birth, the highest officers remained the nobility and knights, but even the officer level underwent a massive transformation. Tournaments in the Holy Roman Empire included foot combat, and the nobility would take their place in the pike square along with the commoners, thus leading by example. Maximilian often wore the armor of a foot soldier and took his place alongside the regular men, even when he was on parade, which inspired far more loyalty than the nobility of other nations commanded. It also provided knowledge, as the nobles who actually stood in such positions better understood their troops, their needs, and their capabilities.

Like the Swiss mercenaries, regiments would be recruited from a local area, thus ensuring that many new recruits knew one another. A *bestallungbrief*, or letter of appointment, was read to potential recruits and outlined the term of service (usually no more than six months), terms of war (whether looting was allowed, for example), size of the regiment, and wages. Regular troops generally earned four guilders a month, which was more than a skilled worker made and more than twice that of an unskilled laborer, although the troops were expected to come with their own kits and pay for their own food.

During this period, agricultural efficiency rose and Europe experienced a population boom, which meant there were plenty of younger sons who would never inherit family farms or shops, and guild laws had become so strict that many apprentices could not take their master's examination and have the chance to set up a trade on their own. Thus, there were many young men who lacked opportunities, and the chance for adventure, travel, and earning good pay all offered strong temptations. As one contemporary writer noted, recruits rallied to the call "like flies in the summer, so that the observer would wonder himself to death, where such a swarm had come from and where it had lain all winter." Of course, pay was a major sticking point, and the records are full of tales of foolish lords who hired Landsknechts and failed to pay them, only to have the mercenaries ditch the campaign and head home, looting as they went.

While the Landsknecht armies were far more democratic than others of their day, there was still some selection based on social class thanks to the requirement of soldiers having to buy their own kits. Even the most basic kit cost around 12 guilders, and with a suit of decent armor costing 16 guilders and a warhorse more than 40, only the wealthy stood the chance of being recruited into the officer corps. Being literate was also necessary for most officer positions.

Between the commoners and the gentry was a middle class who could afford armor and superior weapons but not the horse required of officers. These became *doppelsöldner*, or "double soldiers," who received eight guilders per month instead of the usual four. Their better armor and weapons put them in the front ranks of any formation, which ensured they would bear the brunt of the fighting.

Recruitment was overseen by the *obrist* or colonel, an experienced veteran who was also good with people and was paid 400 guilders a month. This was a handsome sum, but his expenses were high - not only did he have a small train of servants to support, but he had to have the finest weapons and armor, not to mention at least one horse. His main task wasn't to lead the men in battle but to make sure they were cared for in a proper manner. It was his responsibility to get money from the client to pay men's wages, and in case of a shortfall, he often had to pay out of his own pocket to avoid trouble in camp, with the hope that he would later recoup the loss from the client.

The *obirst* also supported a staff, including a chaplain, a translator if needed, a flagbearer, a small personal bodyguard, fifers and drummers, and a *pfenningmeister*, or "penny master." The *pfenningmeister* was one of the most important officers in the army and the one the regular soldiers looked to the most because he was responsible for managing the regiment's money and doling out pay and money for communal expenses.

The regiments varied in size, and it wasn't until the middle of the 16th century that a regiment took on a set character. In the mid-16th century, it was made up of 10 *fähnlein*, literally "banners." Each *fähnlein* had 300-500 men under a captain, who made 40 guilders a month. Often the captain would take on some recruitment responsibilities, going to areas where he was known and recruiting men he thought would make good soldiers. Unlike the colonel, the captain would fight on foot.

Beneath the captain was the ensign, who carried the banner for the *fähnlein* and marched in the center of the pike square, surrounded by the fifers and drummers. These musicians were essential for getting the men to march in time by giving audio cues, the same way the banners provided visual cues. The banner was hugely important as a rallying point and a symbol of group unity and pride, and an ensign wouldn't be able to face his comrades if he allowed the banner to be taken. As if true of all periods of war, the enemy's banner was considered the greatest prize, and there are many tales of ensigns fighting to the death to protect the banner.

A contemporary depiction of Landsknechts with instruments

Below the ensign came the *feldweibel*, or sergeant major, who was generally an older veteran acting as a drillmaster. Moving a pike square in formation was no easy task, so the sergeant major would drill the men regularly to make sure they kept up proper habits. He would be helped by the experienced *doppelsöldner*, which had to have extra armor and good weapons because most would be placed in the front ranks of each file, where the danger was greatest. The *doppelsöldner* at the very front of each file (thus making up the front rank) was called a *rottmeister*. He had the additional duty of representing the men's interests in the *schultheiss* court. Two *gemeinweibel*, or sergeants, marched on either side of the formation to help the *feldweibel* keep it together, while other *doppelsöldner* were scattered throughout the *fähnlein* as a stiffening element for less-experienced soldiers to keep them going in proper formation and to keep them resolute.

There was also a *hurenweibel*, literally "whores' sergeant," who kept the baggage train and camp followers organized. The baggage train was made up of women and underage boys. Besides doing the cooking, much of the carrying, and various menial tasks, they also helped build fortifications. This was unusual in armies of the time because troops usually built the earthworks and filled the gabions - large, open-ended wicker cylinders that were filled with earth and used as quick and cheap protection against bullets - themselves. This inevitably led to extra fatigue before the battle had even started.

Since the Landsknecht had to see to all its own needs, a group of them usually pooled together to pay for a woman to do their cooking, washing, and mending. She might choose to sell other services, as well. She or a young boy would also act as a teamster, taking care of the wagon that carried the tents, bedrolls, cooking pots, and other materials needed for camp life. There was generally a wagon for every 10 soldiers, so the wagon train for a large army could stretch for miles. This meant the *hurenweibel* had a tough job keeping all of the rabble in line and moving along the route of the march. He would also have to weed out the cheats, the sick, and the thieves from among them. It is no surprise that he was generally paid 40 guilders a month, 10 times the salary of a man in the rank-and-file, as his work was constant and vital.

Boys generally acted as assistants to the troops, in the process learning all the martial skills they would need to become Landsknechts in their time. They'd sharpen weapons, clean armor, and practice drills. It certainly would have been a fertile learning environment if they survived, but that was never guaranteed because the baggage trains were often attacked by the enemy, and the ensuing slaughter took its toll. War was unimaginably brutal in those days, and the supposed noncombatants in the baggage train could expect no more mercy than the Landsknechts showed the enemy villages they plundered along the march.

Two other officers were associated with the baggage train: the *quartermeister* and the *proviantmeister*. The *quartermeister* scouted out campsites for the night, as well as billets in towns and villages for the officers. The *proviantmeister* was the "master of provisions" who negotiated with the local population for the sale of food to the men. He had to get a good deal so the men wouldn't grumble, but he could not drive prices so low that they kept the merchants away.

The Landsknecht forces retained a remarkable amount of discipline for the time. A provost would make the rounds of the camp to ensure the men were behaving, and offenders were hauled before the *schultheiss*, a legal expert who handled any cases. When the men signed on, they had to take an oath to obey the articles of war, swearing to God they would not break them. Such oaths were taken seriously in those days, and men feared spiritual repercussions if they broke them. The articles of war included such rules as killing any comrade who retreated without orders or tried to desert. The men were not allowed to hold meetings without the colonel's permission, loot property in friendly territory, or hurt women, children, the elderly, or priests. They were not to loot churches or take the Lord's name in vain. They were also required to attend religious services on a regular basis, for which a regimental chaplain was available. They were also supposed to keep drinking and gambling "within reasonable limits."

Of course, these rules only applied as long as their employer kept up his end of the bargain and paid them regularly. It was generally considered that pay could be up to two weeks late without the agreement being broken, although there are records of the Landsknechts remaining under oath for much longer than that. There are also many cases of the Landsknechts breaking their oaths at the first available opportunity. The stipulation of not hurting women, even in enemy territory, was broken quite frequently, though looting churches was one rule few Landsknechts dared to break, no matter how late their pay.

It is interesting to note that Maximilian put the Landsknechts above civil law, declaring that they could not be tried in a civilian court but only in a military one. This unusual practice did not lead to rampant killing - on the contrary, the Landsknechts were more orderly than most armies in this rough period because they were subject to the strict discipline of military law. Justice was meted out through courts that were open to all, and the courts issued harsh punishments for those who were found guilty. The trial would take place at a court bench set up in camp, and anyone who wanted to attend could do so, but they had to come lightly armed and not disrupt the proceedings.

The military court acted much like a civil one, with a judge and prosecuting and defense attorneys. The defendant was judged by a group of his peers, which was exceedingly unusual for the time and highlighted just how different the Landsknechts were. The jury, which numbered 24 men, had at least half its number made up of men from the ranks, the special and respected *doppelsöldner*, while the other half was composed of ensigns, captains, or sergeants, many of whom would be close to equal the rank of the man under trial. The colonel had veto power over court decisions but had to maintain a balancing act between keeping the order and keeping in the men's good graces.

The provost was one of the most important jobs in the army, and it paid accordingly. When the army was camped and attracted local merchants, he would make sure the merchants were safe. Among a bunch of rough, battle-ready men, it was important that the merchants could conduct business without fear of abuse or intimidation; otherwise, they wouldn't come, and the army would lack essential supplies. In return, the merchants saw to it that the provost remained happy, so he would get a cut of any of their transactions, whether in cash or in kind. Since, like many of the higher officers, he had a train of underlings to support, he often took his cut in the form of food.

The provost had his fingers in many pies and tried to make a profit wherever he could. Even prisoners under arrest and under his guard had to pay for their upkeep. In an army that prided itself on its flamboyant costumes, the provost was one of the most sumptuously dressed, and many of his fine clothes and gold chains were undoubtedly "gifts" from merchants who tagged along for the march.

Associated with the provost was the *scharfrichter*, or executioner. In contrast to the provost, he was rather somberly dressed in a plain red doublet with a red feather in his hat. He carried a heavy executioner's sword with which he beheaded people, and he would carry out his job while the whole army lined up in formation to watch. He was also in the habit of carrying a hangman's noose in his hand.

Landsknecht Culture

The organization of the Landsknechts demonstrated how they were considered separate from society, but this was also enshrined in Imperial law, which made them both attractive and intimidating to the common people. Many young men across the empire must have dreamed of getting away from the daily grind and taking their chances on the battlefield with the Landsknechts. Many a young woman must have dreamed of following along with the army to enjoy their company, as well as their wealth. As in all time periods, there must have been a few women, cunning and hardy, who disguised themselves as men and made a career out of being a Landsknecht. Unfortunately, there are no records of any women who did this, as there are for disguised female soldiers such as Jennie Irene

Hodgers in the American Civil War or Wanda Gertz in World War I. The closest to this period that historians know about is Brita Olofsdotter, a Finnish woman who dressed as a man to serve in the Swedish army. When she was killed in battle in 1569 and her secret was discovered, King John III of Sweden ordered her remaining salary be given to her family, like any man who died in battle.

As with any of society's outsiders, the Landsknechts were also looked upon with a certain amount of fear. Many contemporary paintings and engravings highlight their drunken, riotous behavior, which makes clear that no matter how much discipline the provost and *scharfrichter* tried to instill in their men, there would always be a few rough types who would take what they wanted. Moreover, all the men could be trusted to be loud and brazen, so citizens must have trembled when a Landsknecht army came into town.

The Landsknechts knew they were feared and admired in equal measure, and they set themselves apart with their distinctive dress. In an age where most localities had sumptuary laws, the Landsknechts were free to dress as they wished, and they tried to outdo each other with the flamboyance and outrageousness of their costumes. The men favored bright colors, and often more than one in a garment, either colored stripes or half a pair of hose a different color than the other half. Puffy sleeves were all the rage, as was a strange practice called "slashing" in which cuts were made on the sleeves, bodice, or shoulders to reveal a different colored cloth beneath it. They selected the most colorful, expensive cloth, and silk was quite popular.

An even more unusual practice was to cut off the top part of their hose to leave the thigh bare, and either rolling down the bottom part or keeping it in place with a ribbon tied around the calf. This could be done to both legs or only one of them to heighten the contrast. Why this was done and how the fashion started is a mystery.

Another essential piece of clothing was the codpiece - the bigger the better - often made of a different colored cloth for emphasis. The codpiece was often so large that it could be used to store valuables. The reaction when one of these fellows sauntered into a village, asked the price of a few eggs from a farm girl, and then reached inside his codpiece to pull out a coin can only be imagined.

For headgear, Landsknechts favored a beret with feathers. Peacock feathers were popular, as were expensive imported ostrich feathers. Often, a wealthy Landsknecht would have a whole plumage of feathers on his hat.

Jewelry was popular, as well, and contemporary illustrations show the men with rings and a large number of gold or silver chains. This was not only a way to show off, but it acted as portable property.

   Shirt sleeves were often so baggy as to look ridiculous to modern eyes, and it's fair to wonder if they got in the way while fighting.

An engraving of Ernst Friedrich, Margrave of

Baden-Durlach, wearing Landsknecht dress

Fig. 3. Landsknecht mit Zweihänder (nach D. Hopfer).

A depiction of a Landsknecht

A depiction of a Landsknecht with his wife

During battle, a soldier would leave his most elaborate clothing back at the camp and wear armor or simpler garments instead, not wanting to risk ruining the expensive cloth, not to mention that much of it would be impractical in combat situations. After all, everyone in a thousand-man pike square wore plumes of ostrich feathers, some soldiers in the back ranks would not be able to see anything.

Needless to say, many in the clergy fulminated against such attire, and special focus was put on the codpiece as a sin against propriety. In 1555, Bishop Musculus of Frankfurt wrote in a critical pamphlet, "Our young fellows have their cod-pieces [sic] in front puffed out by the flames and rags of Hell so that the Devil can sit and look out in all directions, causing scandal and creating a bad example, nay, poor, giddy, innocent girls are seduced and enticed thereby."

The Landsknechts were not the first soldiers to don such overly elaborate attire. Swiss mercenaries were known for their fine clothing, and they always searched any town they looted for the best cloth, but as was the case with many battles the two fought, the Landsknechts won the contest to become arguably the most overdressed fighting force in history.

Despite their violent lifestyle and over-the-top fashion, many Landsknechts were also deeply devout. This was a highly religious age, and bitter fights between Catholics and Protestants threatened to tear Europe apart. Even in this sense, the Landsknechts kept apart from mainstream society, and while Emperor Maximilian I was Catholic, the majority of the Landsknechts were Protestant, intermixed with a significant minority of Catholics.

Clergy of both faiths could be found within the army, although contemporary sources say they tended to be poorly educated men who couldn't find better positions elsewhere and had to accept a relatively modest eight guilders a month along with all the hardships of camp life. Nevertheless, the Landsknechts were required to attend religious services on a regular basis and not take the Lord's name in vain. There would also be services before the battle and in honor of those who had fallen. It's safe to assume the troops took some solace in these religious rites, no matter their behavior on other days of the week.

The Landsknechts had a strong sense of group identity, defined just as much by what they were not (civilians, or even worse, the hated Swiss mercenaries). As their list of victories grew, they swelled with pride and saw themselves as the greatest fighting force in Europe, but the Swiss mercenaries did not give up their place gracefully. At the time, the demand for trained mercenaries was at its peak, and there were fortunes to be made with the right patron, so competition between the Landsknechts and Swiss mercenaries grew bitter and often violent. When they found themselves at opposite ends of a battlefield, both sides knew the battle would be brutal. The factions also fought a war of words, creating ballads and poems that told of the heroics of one side while mocking the cowardice and blundering of the other. The printing press was spreading across Europe in the late 15th century, and the public was flooded with broadsheets, the early newspapers of the day. Written on one large sheet and meant to be tacked to a wall, the texts told of battle or some other important event and were more often than not illustrated with a woodblock print. These are some of the best sources historians have for Landsknecht costumes.

At times, however, the Landsknechts and fighters from the Swiss cantons found themselves in the same army. This was inevitable given that local rulers bought the best soldiers they could, and naturally they would order their new recruits to get along while serving under the same banner. This mostly worked since the mercenaries were professionals, and as professionals they knew they had to set aside their differences to preserve their reputation.

The Landsknechts in Battle

The Landsknechts proved themselves early on, but things did not always go well for them. No army is invincible, and the Landsknechts got an early lesson in this hard truth when the famous Black Guard, one of the founding units of Maximilian's new force, was dealt a serious blow on February 17, 1500 at the Battle of Hemmingstedt. On that day, they were not fighting for Maximilian, but for the king of Denmark, who had hired them to put down a peasant rebellion.

Suppressing peasant uprisings was something the Black Guard had done in many places with brutal efficiency, and the peasants of Dithmarschen, a region in western Schleswig-Holstein on the shores of the North Sea, had separated and declared a peasants' republic. This marshy region had always enjoyed a great deal of autonomy and had resisted any attempt to bring them to heel for generations. When the Danish crown demanded the rights to build fortresses in Dithmarschen and collect a hefty tax, the peasants stoutly refused, so the Danish king decided to teach the commoners a lesson.

The Danish army consisted of the 4,000 members of the Black Guard, 2,000 armored cavalry, 1,000 "artillerymen" (almost certainly the majority being armed with handgonnes or early muskets along with several cannons), and 5,000 Frisian commoners. Conversely, the Danish peasants had, at most, 4,000 farmers with poor arms and armor. It's likely that they numbered little more than a thousand, and records are unclear, but they were probably armed like most peasant armies, with spears, halberds, and crossbows. For most, their armor would have been little more than thick leather, perhaps with some metal plates sewn onto it. Some of the wealthier landowners would have had better arms and armor, but they would have been few in number.

Given the mismatch, the Danes and their Landsknecht

mercenaries must have been feeling pretty confident as they marched into battle that day. At most, they expected a brief, one-sided fight, and then some fun ransacking the villages.

First, the army advanced on Meldorf, a large town and the site of Dithmarschen's ruling council meetings, and they faced no resistance. Despite this, the invaders slaughtered the inhabitants, looted the town, and burned it to the ground. With those tasks accomplished, the column advanced toward Heide, the largest town in Dithmarschen, but the army had to march along a single road with low-lying farmland to either side. Up ahead, unbeknownst to the invaders since they had not sent out scouts and the weather was snowy, the road led up a low rise the peasants had fortified.

As they drew closer to the peasants' lines, the rebels opened up a dike sluice to flood the low-lying ground, which would soon become all but impassable. The narrow road led to the peasants' defensive position, a fortified earthwork equipped with guns. These were most likely handgonnes, which by that time were quite common, as well as cheap and easy enough to make that any village blacksmith could turn them out. The peasants also seemed to have had at least one cannon and some arquebusiers.

The attackers spread out with their center advancing on

the road and their flanks to either side, but as they did so, the men on the flanks noticed that the soil was growing increasingly wetter. The horses got bogged down and couldn't move forward, and the footmen struggled along slowly under withering fire. Soon, every place but the road and the mound blocking it was underwater. Horses struggled and fell, and men waded along, suddenly disappearing when they stepped into submerged ditches, the weight of their weapons and armor sucking them down. The men who didn't die this way may have slowly succumbed to hypothermia in the chilly water soaking their legs.

The attacking soldiers reaching the mound escaped this fate, but they found themselves struggling up a muddy slope heavily defended by a determined peasant force. Although the Black Guard fought fiercely, they could make no headway.

Then the peasants counterattacked, using poles to vault over the deep water to strike at the Danes and Landsknechts from the sides. While this sounds odd, pole-vaulting over channels was common practice in the Low Countries well into the 20th century. While the peasants were only lightly armored compared to their foes, this became an advantage as they could maneuver through the boggy areas while the attackers could barely move, and they began to cut down the shivering, almost helpless men.

Initially, the invaders managed to fight them off, and they fought off a second counterattack as well, but they must have been seriously weakened by then. Suffering from heavy casualties, hypothermia, and exhaustion, the attackers could not move forward, and the water kept getting deeper, with the mud becoming more debilitating. The road, too, was getting crowded and increasingly churned up by the trampling boots and hooves, and it wasn't much more passable than the floodplain to either side.

Ultimately, the peasants launched a third counterattack that smashed into both sides of the invading army, and the invaders crumpled in the face of the onslaught. Defeat turned into a rout, with more than half of the attacking force being killed or drowning as they tried to escape. Casualties were especially high among the cavalry and the Landsknechts, who were weighed down by their armor and sucked into the chilly water. The invasion was over, and Dithmarschen would remain an independent republic for another 59 years.

A 20th century painting of the battle

The Battle of Hemmingstedt has gone down in history as a classic case of what can happen if one side underestimates the enemy. It is also a good example of how to use the terrain and unconventional weapons (in this case, a sluice gate) to one's advantage.

In 1503, the Spanish and the French were fighting for dominance in Italy, and on April 21 their two armies clashed at Cerignola in the southern part of the country. The French army, led by Louis d'Armagnac, Duke of Nemours, was a traditional force of 9,000 men, the backbone of which was heavy cavalry and Swiss mercenary pikemen, supported by about 40 cannons. The French cavalry and Swiss infantry both enjoyed formidable reputations, and the French had a long string of victories to their name. Facing them was Spaniard

Gonzalo Fernández de Córdoba, leading some 6,300 men, including more than 3,000 infantry wielding pikes and swords, more than 1,000 arquebusiers, 1,500 light and heavy cavalry, and 20 cannons. Of the infantry, some 2,000 were Landsknechts.

The Spanish arrived at the battlefield first, and they got to pick their terrain: a hill they fortified with a ditch and sharpened stakes. They placed their cannons on the top of the hill and the arquebusiers along the trench. The French Army arrived without its artillery, a common problem at the time because—along with the baggage train—it was the slowest moving part of any force. Commanders often left their artillery train behind, either because they were overly eager to close with the enemy or because they were under time constraints. In the case of Louis d'Armagnac, the former was the case. He surveyed the Spanish earthworks and decided to attack without artillery support.

The French cavalry made three charges against the Spanish lines, but each time, their advance was hampered by the ditch and stakes, and they were cut down by the arquebusiers. During the third assault, Louis d'Armagnac was shot and killed, making him perhaps the first commander to be killed by a handheld firearm.

Louis d'Armagnac

A painting of Gonzalo Fernández de Córdoba being presented with Louis d'Armagnac's body

The Swiss second-in-command then took over and ordered the Swiss infantry to advance. This presented a more serious problem for the defenders as the heavily armored French cavalry had little chance of getting through the earthworks, but the Swiss pikemen were highly disciplined and on foot. The Spanish sent the arquebusiers to the flanks while the Landsknecht infantry defended the center. The Swiss engaged in fierce hand-to-hand fighting against the determined Landsknechts, who had already developed a rivalry with the Swiss. Stopped in their tracks at the earthworks while taking fire from the Spanish arquebusiers on both flanks and being harassed by the Spanish light cavalry, the Swiss ended up withdrawing after taking heavy casualties.

Then the Spanish counterattacked. Both their heavy and light infantry moved in on the disorganized ranks, and mounted Spanish arquebusiers moved quickly into position around the battered French heavy cavalry, dismounting and shooting them down. Only a fraction of the French force managed to escape, although the Swiss were able to hold formation and make a fighting retreat, demonstrating their professionalism even in this critical situation. The Spanish persevered until they came upon the French artillery and supply train, still lumbering toward the battlefield, which they promptly captured. At that time, cannons were still quite expensive, so capturing 40 of them was considered a major windfall. The French lost up to 4,000 men, while the Spanish suffered only about 500 casualties.

Warfare was changing. While the French had hired Swiss pikemen, the bulk of their force remained heavy cavalry, a holdover from the previous century. On the other hand, the Spanish used a blend of pikemen, arquebusiers, and swordsmen working together in an early form of what would become the famous Spanish *tercios*. Military historians often point to Cerignola as the first battle primarily won by firearms. The French were looking back while the Spanish were looking forward.

Although the Landsknechts were not a pivotal unit in the battle - they were brought into play only after the French were seriously weakened - they did fare well and faced off against the Swiss pike squares. This major battle was one of many in which the new Landsknecht units developed their formidable reputation.

During the Landsknechts' heyday, there was constant warfare in Italy. A patchwork of different states backed by larger powers, there was always a succession to dispute or a broken treaty to avenge. The Italian Wars, as they were collectively called, stretched from 1494-1559 and provided regular work for both the Landsknechts and their rivals, the Swiss.

One important battle in this series of connected wars was fought at Ravenna in northern Italy on April 11, 1512. The French, led by the popular and talented general Gaston de Foix, were besieging the city held by the Papal States. At that time, the pope was aligned with the Spanish, who had an army nearby that came to Ravenna's aid. The French knew they were coming, so they left a skeleton force behind to keep the people of Ravenna bottled up behind their walls while moving south to confront the Spanish.

The Spanish camped just south of the Ronco River. Impatient to enter battle, de Foix crossed the river and moved to attack their fortified camp. The order of battle is unclear, as are the numbers of men on each side, but it appears that the French had about 25,000 men, including 1,700 French men-at-arms (heavy cavalry), 2,000 light Italian cavalry, 9,500 Landsknechts, 8,000 French archers and pikemen, and 4,000 Italian infantry. The Spanish had around 16,000 men and enjoyed the protection of entrenchments and war wagons. These were two-wheeled carts with a protective wooden shield and row of small cannon called "organ guns" that could keep up a withering fire. Their forces included 1,700 men-at-arms, 1,500 Spanish light cavalry, an unknown number of mounted Italian arquebusiers, and a mixture of Spanish infantry and Papal footmen.

Both sides had a considerable number of artillery pieces, and the battle started with an artillery duel. This opening move, which would soon become standard in warfare, was quite new, so much so that the Battle of Ravenna might have been the first in which an extensive artillery duel was used. The French concentrated their fire on the fortified camp. While the infantry among the defenders was able to hide in the entrenchments to avoid the worst of the fire, the men-at-arms, ordered to remain on their horses, suffered heavy losses. The Spanish aimed their guns at the attacking infantry who were out in the open and were soon badly cut up. The French crossbowmen, shaken by the fire, looked about to break and run for the rear, and the Landsknechts had to prod them with their pikes to keep them in position.

The French managed to work some artillery behind the camp and fire a hit from the other side, although some of the cannonballs flew over the camp to hit the French lines. Another two heavy guns were kept north of the river to hit the camp from that side.

The Spanish cavalry could endure this no more and emerged from the camp to charge at the French cavalry. A long melee ensued with the Spanish eventually breaking and fleeing the field, pursued by the bulk of the French cavalry.

As this was happening, the Landsknechts and French infantry stormed the fortified camp, which did not go well. Fired at from point-blank range by the organ guns and handgonnes, and also hampered by the earthworks, the Landsknecht pike square became disorderly, and the Spanish rushed between the pikes to slash at the Germans with swords. The fight was long and bitter, with the French and Germans taking the worst of the casualties.

The French cavalry returned from pursuing the Spanish cavalry to hit the Spaniards from all sides. They soon broke and fled, leaving most of their number behind as dead or wounded.

Sadly for the French, Gaston de Foix fell near the end of his victory. The loss of their commander was a serious blow for morale, and what had been a victory turned out to be the end of the campaign. The French attacked Ravenna again and sacked it, but after being faced with a fresh, larger relief force coming to attack them, they moved out of Italy.

A woodcut depicting the battle

Though the French had been kicked out of the country, they would soon return. The Swiss had helped place Massimiliano Sforza on the throne as Duke of Milan at the end of 1512, but the French wanted Milan for themselves, so they returned to northern Italy the following year. In northwest Italy on the opposite side of the Alps from France, the city was a barrier to further penetrating the peninsula, and without controlling it, the French could not move farther south without threatening their rear. Furthermore, the Dukedom of Milan was a prosperous state in its own right, a prize well worth the fight. Milan was also quite close to the Swiss Confederacy border, and the Swiss wanted a duke who shared their interests. Thus, Milan became a flashpoint between the French and the Swiss for much of the early 16th century.

The French marched over the Alps, no small feat with heavily armored men and lumbering artillery, and moved into the Dukedom of Milan to besiege the city of Novara and its garrison of Swiss mercenaries. In a series of forced marches, a Swiss force rushed to relieve the city before it fell.

The two sides met on June 6, 1513, and this time, the French and their Landsknecht mercenaries faced Milan's forces and their Swiss Confederate mercenaries. The French fielded an army of 1,200 heavy cavalry, 600 light cavalry, 14,000 infantry, 6,000 Landsknechts, 2,500 bowmen, and 28 cannons, facing a force of mostly Swiss pikemen. Sources vary as to their numbers, ranging from 11,000-20,000, but the sources all agree that the Swiss possessed an inferior force, both in number and branches of services. The Swiss notably lacked significant cavalry and artillery.

The Swiss advanced quickly, managing a deft maneuver to go at the French from multiple directions. The French artillery did deadly work against the packed troops, taking down 700 men in just three minutes, but then the Swiss closed in on the enemy lines, and with that the tide of battle shifted. At first, the Landsknecht pike squares held against the Swiss, but the Swiss encircled the French camp, hemming in the French cavalry so it couldn't properly deploy. The Swiss captured the French guns, and upon finding themselves attacked on all sides, the French and German units broke one by one.

A general slaughter ensued, with the Swiss descending on their hated rivals and showing them no mercy. The French headed north in full retreat, and without any cavalry to pursue, the Swiss could not harry them properly, but they did follow them all the way to Dijon. The French king eventually paid them to leave France, but either way, the French were once again kicked out of Italy.

This was not the end of the French's designs. They soon returned to Italy, and the Landsknechts had their revenge at the Battle of Marignano on September 13-14, 1515. Once again, the French moved in to contest control of Milan, and this time they were led by King Francis I (r.

1515-1547). The king was young (the battle started the day after his 21st birthday), had just been crowned in January of that year, and was eager to prove himself to his people and Europe as a whole.

A painting of the French king at the battle

One of the most significant battles of the early 16th century—and the one that made the young king's career—was never meant to take place. The Swiss were outnumbered and tired after many years of campaigning. They had collected a good amount of booty and wanted to go home. The captains of the various Swiss units debated the issue, and the majority won out, making terms with King Francis to give him Milan in return for safe passage back to Switzerland.

Francis retired to his camp, content with having scored an easy major victory. He was trying on a new set of armor when he received some stunning news: a large Swiss force was marching against him.

Unbeknownst to him, a second Swiss Army had come over the mountains from Switzerland, eager to fight. They were egged on by Cardinal Matthäus Schiner, the Papal commander. The Papal States were still aligned with Milan and the Swiss at the time. Soon, some of the Swiss units in Milan had joined in, and they marched hurriedly out to attack the French camp.

Despite the reinforcements, the Swiss still had numerical inferiority, having 22,000 infantry and only 200 cavalry. There is no record they had any artillery. They faced a French force of 3,000 gendarmes (heavy cavalry of noble birth and expert training), 19,000 landsknechts, 10,000 other infantry, and 72 cannons.

The Swiss were undaunted. They had faced down larger forces before by sending in pike formations at full charge, a difficult maneuver that was testament to their training. Since the artillery of the time was slow to reload and not terribly accurate, it would only get one wild shot at a moving target before the Swiss closed.

The two sides met on open, featureless ground near the town of Marignano. Despite their surprise, the French got into the order of battle quickly enough to face the Swiss. They placed their artillery, then considered the most advanced in Europe, in the center, where it could sweep the open field and protect both flanks. Knowing the Swiss might go for the guns, King Francis posted the Landsknecht Black Guard next to them.

The Swiss came into the battle piecemeal as the sun was already low in the western sky. The first pike square to arrive, slightly ahead of the main body, decided to launch their attack while there was still light, and they ran right for the French guns.

As before, the Swiss passed bravely through the artillery fire to push back the Landsknechts, capturing a few guns. Their victory was short-lived, as the gendarmes hit them on the side and chased them all the way back to the main body of Swiss just as they were assembling on the field. The larger Swiss force held their ground, and the gendarmes, faced with a wall of pike points, were forced to retreat.

Now, the sun had set, and with moonlight as their guide, the Swiss charged again and again, only to be pushed back by the Landsknechts and the French cavalry. The fighting seesawed until the moon set, and darkness brought an end to the battle.

At the crack of dawn the next day, the two armies resumed their bloody work. It was more or less a repeat of the day before, with the Swiss charging the guns, suffering heavy losses to get in close, and pushing the Black Guard back only to be pushed back in counterattacks by the Landsknechts and French cavalry.

Both sides suffered heavy losses, but the smaller Swiss Army could less afford them. What finally tipped the balance was the arrival of the Venetians, who were French allies. Seven hundred heavy cavalry rode into the fray with 8,000 infantry coming up behind them.

The Swiss could not face such odds, and they retreated before the Venetian infantry could deploy on the battlefield. The number of losses is unclear, but various sources say the French suffered 3,000-8,000 casualties, while the Swiss lost 8,000-14,000 men. Even the most modest estimate has the Swiss losing more than a third of their forces.

The French gained Milan, and the reputation of the young King Francis was made. The French sent Massimiliano Sforza into exile with a generous pension—the nobility generally treated its own with courtesy, and it was best to keep one's formal rivals from being too resentful. The Swiss signed a peace treaty with France, forever giving up their Italian interests. This and the divisions created by religious debates between Catholics and Protestants back in Switzerland meant that the Swiss would play less and less of a role in European warfare and politics in the years to come.

A depiction of the Swiss and Landsknechts fighting in the battle

A contemporary depiction of the battlefield drawn by Urs Graf, a Swiss mercenary

King Francis fought another decisive engagement at Pavia in northern Italy on February 24, 1525. Once again, the fight was over control of Milan, but in the interim, the Holy Roman Empire, backed by Spain, England, and the Papal States, had taken Milan, and King Francis wished to get it back. The French forces, led by King Francis I, included 17,000 infantry, 6,500 cavalry, and 53 cannons. Of the infantry, 6,000 were French, 8,000 were Swiss, and there was a 9,000-man force of mixed Germans and Italians, including 4,000 Landsknecht pikemen who had hired themselves out to Francis even though the king was fighting the Holy Roman Empire.

This huge force moved through Lombardy, sweeping aside smaller Imperial forces and taking Milan. Next, they descended on the city of Pavia, where Spanish General Antonio de Leyva commanded an Imperial garrison of about 9,000 men. Several French assaults failed, and King Francis settled in for a long siege, waiting for the garrison to run out of food.

Coming to the city's aid was an Imperial force of about 19,000 infantry, including 12,000 German Landsknechts, 5,000 Spanish, 3,000 Italians, 4,000 cavalry, and 17 cannons. Most of the men were Spanish and were led by Charles de Lannoy, the renegade Duke of Bourbon, and the Spaniard Fernando de Avalos, the Marquis of Pescara. The bulk of the infantry were pikemen and arquebusiers.

They came upon the French force at night, camped within a walled hunting park that provided them some protection, but the Imperial relief force was able to break through the wall undetected, and the fighting soon began. There were several confusing clashes in the dark before the sun rose, and both sides got into some order as daylight broke. At dawn, the main French cavalry charged the Imperial lines, and the Imperial infantry was able to lure the French cavalry into a cramped area surrounded by woods. Unable to maneuver, the French soon found themselves surrounded by Landsknecht pikemen and Spanish arquebusiers. The pikemen hemmed the horsemen in even further, the concentrated gunfire of expert Spanish arquebusiers all but wiped out the cavalry, and King Francis was taken prisoner. In the meantime, the garrison in Pavia made a sortie and overran the smaller force that had been left to man the French siege lines.

This battle ensured that the Holy Roman Empire would dominate Italy, while King Francis was forced to sign the humiliating Treaty of Madrid on January 14, 1526, making many hefty concessions before he was allowed to go free.

A depiction of the Battle of Pavia

The Decline of the Landsknechts

Military historians look at the Battle of Pavia as a watershed moment. After this battle, no commander could ignore the power of a well-trained force of arquebusiers and pikemen. The era of pike and shot warfare had truly begun.

Over the next several decades, the Landsknechts served all over Europe, from Hungary to Scandinavia to Italy. In one major campaign, they even crossed the Mediterranean to fight in North Africa. Emperor Charles V (r. 1519-1530) was worried about Ottoman expansion into the western Mediterranean. Sultan Suleiman the Magnificent (r. 1520-1566), sent a large fleet headed by pirate Captain Hayreddin Barbarossa to take Tunis in 1534. From this port, the Turkish fleet could threaten Europe's shipping and its coasts.

North African piracy was extensive at the time, with pirates from Tunis, Algiers, Tripoli, and a number of smaller ports harassing European shipping and raiding European coastal villages to take people away as slaves. The North African slave market was thriving, and European slaves fetched a high price. The men were generally worked to death in public building projects or mines, while the women ended up as sex-slaves. With such a strong Muslim fleet in the area, the raids only got worse.

Charles was backed by the Knights of Malta, Portugal, and the Papal States, as well as the local Hafsid dynasty, who the Turks had kicked out of Tunis. At great expense, Charles assembled a huge fleet of nearly 400 ships to carry some 60,000 soldiers, sailors, and camp followers, including 8,000 Landsknechts, to attack the city.

It proved a grueling campaign right from the start. Landsknecht soldier Niklaus Guldi wrote an account of his adventures in the flotilla, complaining that the food was inedible, the bread had been stored in Naples for years and was full of worms and moths, the water was foul, and the pork was in an advanced state of putrefaction.

The fleet arrived at Goletta, the harbor of Tunis, on 15 June. The ships blockaded the harbor and the infantry with the Landsknechts leading the way, and they stormed Goletta after a month-long siege during which the Turks made several sorties. Once the city was taken, the emperor, who had gone along on the campaign, released 1,200 Christian slaves and sent them back home to Europe before marching on Tunis.

The Turks attacked again, working their way around the army to fall on the baggage train, and killing many women and boys before they could be driven off. The Turks then withdrew, and the Imperial advance continued. Guldi recorded that the weather was so hot that "the armored men nearly suffocated and thought they would die of the heat, and when one went to help the other by loosening the armor, he would burn his fingers on the metal."

When they finally arrived at Tunis, they found that Barbarossa had retreated. When he had fought the emperor at Goletta, the slaves in Tunis revolted, killed the guards, and took over the city.

The Landsknechts tried to march into the city, but the new defenders panicked and fought back, which proved a disastrous mistake. The Landsknechts and other Imperial troops, infuriated at being attacked when they thought they'd be greeted as liberators, stormed the city, slaughtering tens of thousands of inhabitants and sacking it. The streets were filled with bodies of men, women, and children, and everything valuable was stripped from the buildings. The stench of the bodies was so bad that the army had to flee the city to camp four miles away at the port of Radès; such was the barbarity of war in those days. Hafsid ruler Muley Hassan was put back on the throne of Tunis as a puppet to the Holy Roman Empire, but he had little left over to rule.

The Ottoman expansion into Europe was checked, but Europe was changing by the mid-16th century, and rulers established a firmer hold on their territories. This and the rise of trade made it possible to raise taxes and support larger standing armies. The nobility never wanted to hire mercenaries, who could sometimes be unreliable and prone to looting in friendly territory, especially after their term of service was finished, but the rise of an urban class and a more prosperous and efficient countryside ensured there was an excess of available labor to join the military. Thus, mercenaries were less needed and thereby less valued. It is interesting to note that four guilders a month, the typical pay for the Landsknecht in the late 15th century, was still the regular pay in the middle of the 16th century, more than two generations later, despite a great deal of inflation. The same number of mercenaries competed for fewer jobs that paid less.

There were military changes, as well. While the Landsknecht had become a major force in European warfare, they never entirely pushed their rivals, the Swiss, off the center stage. Both groups would fade away in the middle of the 16th century, the Swiss due to internal strife and the Landsknechts because a new force had risen in the West by using innovative tactics that would take the pike and shot era to the next level. These were the Spanish *tercios*, a combination of infantry, arquebusiers, and swordsmen that became the main units in the Spanish armies starting around 1500. The *tercios* were originally supposed to have been made up of 3,000 men, although there were usually 1,500, and they got their name (tercio means "third" in Spanish) by being composed of 33% arquebusiers, 33% pikemen, and 33% men armed with swords, javelins, and bucklers. The sword-and-buckler men had been around for some time and were another mercenary group who plied their trade throughout Europe.

In battle, pikemen formed a hollow square or rectangle, with the swordsmen inside and the arquebusiers in smaller units deployed around the square, especially at the corners. This allowed for a range of firepower combined with a good defense against cavalry. Several of these squares were deployed in a staggered, "dragon-toothed" formation, with the front rank of one unit in line with the back rank of the preceding unit. This allowed for enfilade fire and the ability to flank enemy formations, something the Swiss and the Landsknechts had not done. The swordsmen were soon replaced with more pikemen because it was found that the swordsmen didn't get into hand-to-hand combat enough, and their javelins weren't of much use on the modern battlefield. In time, the arquebusiers were eventually replaced with musketeers, and as firearms improved in accuracy, range, and stopping power throughout this period, the number of musketeers grew in relation to the number of pikemen.

As they began to enjoy success after success, the *tercios* dominated the battlefield, and the Landsknechts and the Swiss faded into history, but mercenaries continued to be used by nation-states well into more modern times. In the middle of the 20th century, they were commonly found in the African and Latin American revolutions and interstate wars, often in the role of strengthening and training local troops. These tended to be motley crews of individual adventurers brought temporarily under the command of charismatic leaders such as Mad Mike Hoare. Although their organization and staying power cannot be compared to the Landsknechts, early 21st century mercenaries are more professional than ever, working for international corporations often called private military companies, such as Executive Outcomes and Blackwater USA. These private military companies have been a growth industry in recent years, seeing service in all corners of the globe and even being hired by superpowers like the United States to work in crisis zones such as Iraq.

If anything, it appears mercenaries may be enjoying a new Renaissance.

Online Resources

Other books about medieval history by Charles River Editors

Other books about the Landsknechts on Amazon

Further Reading

Appelbaum, Stanley. *The Triumph of Maximilian I.* Mineola, New York: Dover Publications, Inc., 1964.

Bennet, Matthew, et al. *Fighting Techniques of the*

Medieval World AD 500-AD 1500: Equipment, Combat Skills and Tactics. Staplehurst, Kent: Spellmount Ltd, 2005.

Bennett, Matthew and Christer Jorgensen, Michael Pavkovic, Rob S. Rice, Frederick S. Schneid, Chris Scott. *Fighting Techniques of the Early Modern World 1500-1763.* London: Amber Books Ltd., 2005.

Charles River Editors and Sean McLachlan. *Warfare in the Middle Ages: The History of Medieval Military and Siege Tactics.* Charles River Editors: 2015.

Charles River Editors and Sean McLachlan. *Warfare in the Era of Pike and Shot: The History and Legacy of the Military Strategies that Ushered in Modern Warfare.* Charles River Editors: 2017.

Davies, Jonathan. *The Medieval Cannon 1326-1494.* Oxford: Osprey Publishing, 2019.

DeVries, Kelly. *Medieval Military Technology.* Peterborough, Ontario: Broadview Press Ltd, 1992.

Hale, J. R.. *War and Society in Renaissance Europe 1450–1620.* Stroud, United Kingdom: Sutton Publishing, 1998.

Hall, Bert. *Weapons and Warfare in Renaissance Europe.* London: The John Hopkins University Press,

2001.

Hogg, O. F. G.. *Artillery: Its Origin, Heyday, and Decline.* London: C. Hurst & Co, 1970.

McLachlan, Sean. *Medieval Handgonnes: The First Black Powder Infantry Weapons.* Oxford: Osprey Publishing, 2010.

Miller, Artur Maximilian. *The Landsknechts.* Botley, United Kingdom: Osprey Publishing, 1976

Miller, Douglas, and Embleton, Gerry. *The Swiss at War 1300–1500.* Oxford: Osprey Publishing, 1998.

Nicolle, David. *Italian Medieval Armies 1300–1500.* Oxford: Osprey Publishing, 1983.

Nicolle, David. *Medieval Warfare Source Book, vols I & II.* London: Arms and Armour Press, 1995.

Richards, John. *Landsknecht Soldier 1486-1560.* Botley, United Kingdom: Osprey Publishing, 2002.

Roberts, Keith. *Pike and Shot Tactics 1590-1660.* Osprey Publishing Ltd.: Oxford, 2010.

Free Books by Charles River Editors

We have brand new titles available for free most days of the week. To see which of our titles are currently free, click on this link.

Discounted Books by Charles River Editors

We have titles at a discount price of just 99 cents everyday. To see which of our titles are currently 99 cents, click on this link.